SORRENTO
TRAVEL GUIDE
2024-2025

Your Ultimate Travel Companion to Adventure, Culture, and Scenic Beauty in the Sorrento, Italy

Robert Charles

Copyright © 2024, Robert Charles

All rights reserved. No part of this publication may be reproduced, distributed, or transmitted in any form or by any means, including photocopying, recording, or other electronic or mechanical methods, without the prior written permission of the publisher, except in the case of brief quotations embodied in critical reviews and certain other noncommercial uses permitted by copyright law.

TABLE OF CONTENTS

INTRODUCTION

CHAPTER ONE: Introduction to Sorrento
- Sorrento: Quick Facts and Statistics
- Brief History of Sorrento
- Geography and Climate
- Getting to Sorrento
- Local Transportation

CHAPTER TWO: Planning Your Trip
- Choosing the Right Time to Visit
- Setting Your Budget
- Accommodation Options
- Creating an Itinerary
- Travel Essentials and Packing Tips

CHAPTER THREE: Exploring Sorrento Neighborhoods
- Sorrento's Old Town and Historic Center

- Marina Grande and the Fishing Village
- Sant'Agnello and the Coastal Retreat
- Piano di Sorrento and the Lemon Groves

CHAPTER FOUR: Must-See Attractions

- Piazza Tasso
- Amalfi Coast Road Trip
- Sorrento Cathedral (Cattedrale dei Santi Filippo e Giacomo)
- Museo Correale di Terranova
- Capri Island Excursion
- Pompeii and Herculaneum

CHAPTER FIVE: Experiencing Sorrento's Culture

- Sorrento's Culinary Scene
- Traditional Sorrentine Cuisine
- Festivals and Events
- Arts and Music in Sorrento
- Local Arts and Crafts

CHAPTER SIX: Outdoor Adventures and Recreation
- Sorrento's Beaches and Water Activities
- Hiking in the Sorrento Peninsula
- Exploring Mount Vesuvius
- Golfing near Sorrento
- Island Hopping in the Gulf of Naples
- Day Trips to Positano and Ravello

CHAPTER SEVEN: Sorrento for Every Traveler
- Family-Friendly Activities
- Sorrento for Romance
- Sorrento for Seniors
- Sorrento for Tourists
- Sorrento for Students
- Solo Travel Tips and Safety

CHAPTER EIGHT: Practical Information and Resources
- Money and Currency
- Language and Communication
- Safety and Health Tips

- Sustainable Travel in Sorrento
- Useful Contacts and Emergency Numbers

APPENDIX
- Useful Travel Resources
- Italian Phrases and Pronunciation Guide

Map to Sorrento

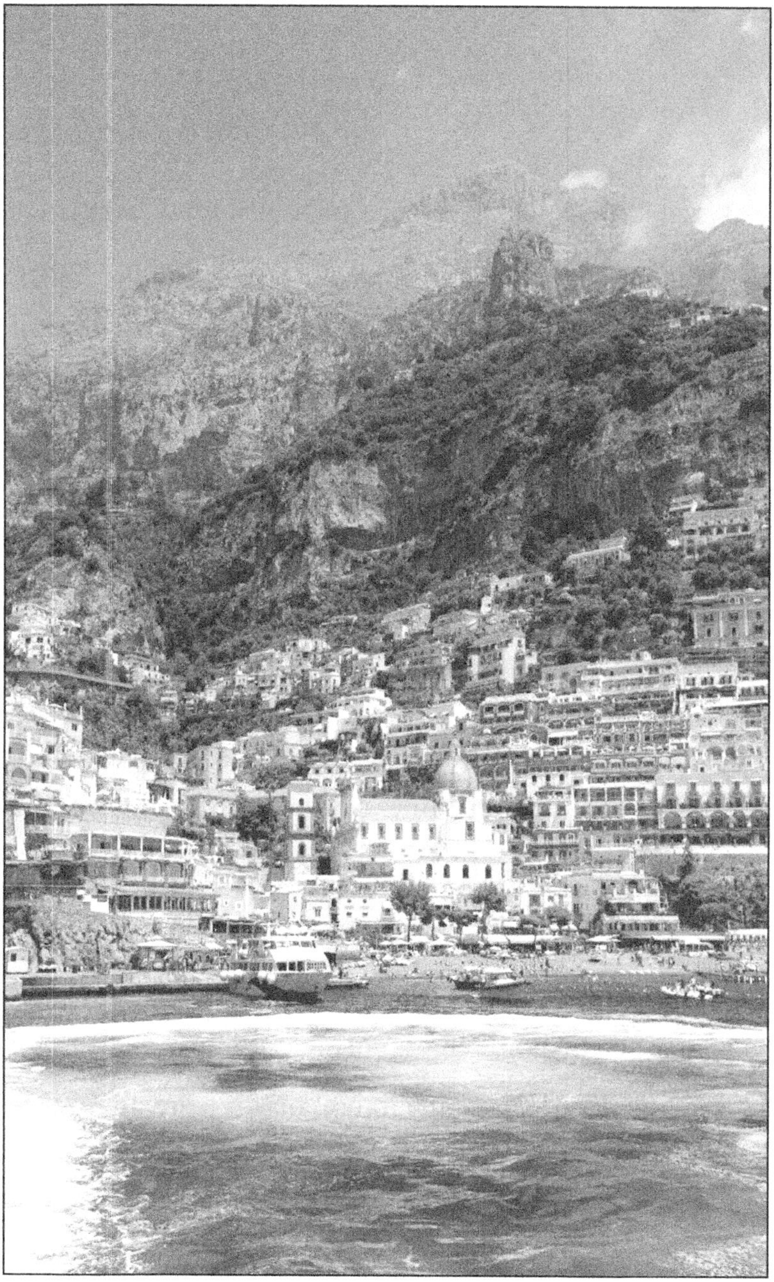

INTRODUCTION

As I pen down these words, I'm transported back to the sun-drenched cliffs and azure waters of Sorrento, Italy—a place where every corner whispers tales of history, romance, and unbridled beauty. Imagine standing on the terrace of a charming café, the gentle sea breeze brushing against your face, as you gaze out over the breathtaking Bay of Naples. This is Sorrento, a destination that feels like stepping into a postcard.

I still remember my first visit to this enchanting town. It was a warm summer evening, and as I strolled through the narrow cobblestone streets, the aroma of freshly baked pizza and the sweet scent of lemon blossoms filled the air. The golden glow of the setting sun bathed the town in a magical light, making the colorful buildings and bustling piazzas look like they were straight out of a dream.

One of my fondest memories is of the Marina Grande, the old fishing village of Sorrento. Here, time seems to stand still. The vibrant fishing boats bobbing gently in the water, the laughter of locals mingling with the clinking of glasses from nearby trattorias, and the delicious seafood dishes prepared with the catch of the day—it all creates an atmosphere that's both lively and intimate. I found myself losing track of time, captivated by the simplicity and beauty of life by the sea.

Then there's the heart of Sorrento, Piazza Tasso, where the energy of the town truly comes alive. By day, it's a bustling hub filled with shops, cafes, and gelaterias, where you can savor the creamiest gelato you've ever tasted. By night, it transforms into a lively gathering place, with music filling the air and laughter echoing through the streets. It's here that I experienced the true spirit of Sorrento—a blend of warmth, joy, and an unspoken invitation to become a part of its story.

Venturing beyond the town, the Amalfi Coast beckons with its dramatic cliffs and winding roads, each turn revealing a new panorama more stunning than the last. I'll never forget the drive along the coast, the thrill of the narrow roads, and the awe-inspiring views that took my breath away. And of course, no visit to Sorrento is complete without a trip to the Isle of Capri, where the Blue Grotto's shimmering waters create a surreal and unforgettable experience.

Sorrento is also a gateway to rich history. The ancient ruins of Pompeii and Herculaneum lie just a short train ride away, offering a poignant glimpse into the past. Walking through these archaeological sites, I felt a deep connection to the stories of those who lived there centuries ago.

In this guide, I invite you to join me on a journey through Sorrento, to uncover the hidden gems and iconic landmarks that make this town a must-visit destination. You'll find tips on the best places to eat, where to stay, and how to make the most of your time in this Mediterranean paradise.

Whether you're a first-time traveler or a seasoned explorer, this guide is designed to help you experience Sorrento in all its glory, with practical advice and insider tips that will make your trip unforgettable.

So, pack your bags, bring your sense of adventure, and get ready to fall in love with Sorrento. Let the pages of this book be your passport to a place where dreams meet reality, and every moment is a beautiful memory in the making. Welcome to Sorrento—your next great adventure awaits.

CHAPTER ONE:
Introduction to Sorrento

Sorrento: Quick Facts and Statistics

Sorrento, an enchanting town on Italy's southwestern coast, is a dreamy destination known for its breathtaking vistas, rich history, and friendly Mediterranean environment. Before commencing on your journey to this interesting location, you should educate yourself with some quick facts and figures.

- Location: Sorrento is situated in the Campania region of Italy, perched on the stunning Sorrentine Peninsula. This remarkable town overlooks the mesmerizing Bay of Naples and provides a gateway to the breathtaking Amalfi Coast. It's strategically located, making it an ideal starting point for exploring the surrounding treasures of southern Italy.

- Population: Sorrento has a population of roughly 15,297 people. While it might not be a bustling metropolis, the town's charm and attractions draw countless tourists year-round, adding vibrancy and diversity to its population.

- Economy: Sorrento's economy is primarily driven by tourism, thanks to its incredible natural beauty, rich culture, and delightful cuisine. Visitors flock here to indulge in the local products, such as limoncello, olive oil, and beautifully crafted ceramics. Fishing and agriculture also play significant roles in the local economy.

- Time Zone: Sorrento operates on Central European Time (CET), which is UTC+1, during the standard time, and Central European Summer Time (CEST), which is UTC+2, during daylight saving time (from the last Sunday in March to the last Sunday in October). Make sure to adjust your timekeeping accordingly if you're traveling from a different time zone.

- Education: Sorrento boasts a selection of educational institutions, ranging from primary schools to secondary schools. The town's commitment to education ensures that local children receive a well-rounded education. However, for higher education and specialized fields of study, students may need to travel to nearby cities such as Naples.

- Government: Sorrento operates as a commune within the Metropolitan City of Naples. Like many Italian towns and cities, it has a local government responsible for municipal affairs, with an elected mayor overseeing the administration.

Brief History of Sorrento

Sorrento's history spans millennia, with influences from numerous civilizations leaving their mark on this gorgeous town. A little historical study will help you better comprehend Sorrento's cultural diversity.

- Ancient Origins: The history of Sorrento can be traced back to ancient times. The region was initially inhabited by the Oscan-Samnite people before coming under Roman rule in the 4th century BC. The Romans recognized Sorrento's strategic importance and turned it into a thriving resort town.

- Medieval and Renaissance Periods: During the medieval era, Sorrento was a part of the Duchy of Naples. The town experienced significant growth and prosperity as it became a thriving maritime center. Trade, fishing, and agriculture formed the backbone of its economy.

- Foreign Invasions: Over the centuries, Sorrento faced various invasions and dominations, including the Byzantine Empire, Saracen raids, and Norman conquests. These influences left a lasting impact on the town's architecture, culture, and traditions.

- Modern Era: In the 19th century, Sorrento began to gain popularity as a tourist destination, especially among the British aristocracy. The advent of the railway system in the late 19th century made it more accessible, and Sorrento continued to flourish as a favorite holiday spot.

- World War II and Post-war Reconstruction: Sorrento, like many Italian towns, experienced the hardships of World War II. After the war, the town underwent a period of reconstruction and tourism began to thrive again, setting the stage for the modern, bustling Sorrento we know today.

Geography and Climate

Sorrento's attractiveness stems mostly from its location and climate. Perched on the Sorrentine Peninsula's cliffs, the town offers stunning views and a one-of-a-kind coastal experience.

- Geography: Sorrento is beautifully positioned overlooking the Bay of Naples, with the grand silhouette of Mount Vesuvius standing tall on the horizon. The town is embraced by rugged cliffs that dive into the sea, offering stunning panoramic views of the Tyrrhenian Sea. Sorrento's location also serves as a perfect gateway to explore the Amalfi Coast, an area renowned for its dramatic cliffs and picturesque villages.

- Climate: Sorrento enjoys a Mediterranean climate, characterized by mild, wet winters and hot, dry summers. Here's a more detailed breakdown of Sorrento's climate:

- Spring (March to May): Spring in Sorrento is a delight. The temperatures are comfortably warm, and the surrounding countryside bursts into bloom with colorful flowers. It's an excellent time for outdoor activities and sightseeing.

- Summer (June to August): The summer months are the peak tourist season. Expect long, sun-drenched days with temperatures ranging from 25°C to 30°C (77°F to 86°F). The sea is invitingly warm for swimming and water-based adventures.

- Autumn (September to November): Autumn is another fantastic time to visit Sorrento. The weather remains pleasant, and the summer crowds begin to dwindle. This is a perfect season for exploring historical sites and enjoying outdoor dining.

- Winter (December to February): Winters in Sorrento are mild but can be damp, with temperatures averaging between 10°C and 15°C (50°F to 59°F). While it's the off-season for tourists, it's an ideal time to enjoy a quieter, more authentic Sorrento experience.

Sorrento's climate makes it a year-round destination, so you can choose the time that suits your preferences and travel plans.

Getting to Sorrento

Reaching Sorrento is an adventure in and of itself, as you travel through the breathtaking Italian scenery. Here are several important ways to travel to this charming town.

1. By Air: The nearest major airport to Sorrento is Naples International Airport, also known as Capodichino Airport (NAP). From the airport, you have several options to reach Sorrento:

- Shuttle Bus: The Curreri Viaggi shuttle bus service operates between the airport and Sorrento. The journey takes approximately 1.5 hours and is a convenient and affordable option.

- Private Transfer: You can arrange for a private transfer or taxi from the airport to Sorrento. This is a more comfortable but slightly more expensive option.

2. By Train: Sorrento is connected to Naples and other parts of Italy by a scenic and efficient rail network. The

Circumvesuviana train line runs from Naples to Sorrento, and the journey offers picturesque views of the coastline. The Sorrento train station is conveniently located near the town center.

3. By Car: If you're traveling by car, you can rent one at the airport or other major cities in Italy. The drive to Sorrento is an opportunity to explore the stunning Amalfi Coast, but be prepared for narrow and winding roads.

4. By Sea: You can also reach Sorrento by sea, with ferries and hydrofoils operating from Naples, Capri, and other nearby coastal towns. Arriving by sea offers a unique perspective of the town's dramatic cliffs and coastline.

5. By Bus: Sorrento is well-connected by bus services to Naples and other nearby towns. It's an economical option for travelers, but the journey might take longer due to traffic.

No matter which mode of transportation you choose, the journey to Sorrento is an experience in itself, with every route offering stunning views and a sense of anticipation for the adventures that await.

Local Transportation

Sorrento's small size and gorgeous streets make it an ideal walking destination. However, if you wish to explore beyond the town center or visit surrounding sites, there are several means of local transportation accessible to make your trip more convenient.

1. Buses: Sorrento has an extensive bus network that connects the town to other destinations in the region. The orange buses of the Circumvesuviana company are a common sight and can take you to nearby towns such as Positano and Amalfi. Be sure to check the bus schedules and routes as they can be subject to changes.

2. Trains: The Circumvesuviana train line connects Sorrento to Naples and other towns in the region. It's a convenient option for day trips or longer journeys. The train station is located near the town center, making it easy to access.

3. Taxis: Taxis are readily available in Sorrento, and you can either hail one on the street or find them at designated taxi stands. Taxis are a comfortable but more expensive option for getting around town or to nearby destinations.

4. Boats and Ferries: Sorrento's proximity to the sea means that you can use boats and ferries to explore the coastal towns and islands. This is a delightful way to travel, offering stunning views and a unique perspective on the region.

5. Funivia (Cable Car): For easy access to the beach at Marina Grande, you can take the funivia, a cable car that

connects the town center to the waterfront. The short ride provides panoramic views of the bay.

6. Walking: Sorrento's town center is best explored on foot. It's a delightful experience to wander through its charming streets, discovering hidden gems, local shops, and quaint cafes.

With these local transportation options, you can easily explore Sorrento and its surrounds, making the most of your trip to this charming coastal town. Sorrento provides a multitude of opportunities to appreciate its beauty and culture, whether you're strolling through the lovely streets, taking a bus to a nearby town, or taking a scenic boat excursion.

CHAPTER TWO:
Planning Your Trip

Planning a vacation to Sorrento is an exciting activity, and careful planning ensures that your visit is seamless, fun, and memorable. In this chapter, I'll walk you through the many stages of preparing your Sorrento journey, such as determining the best time to come, selecting a budget, researching lodging alternatives, building a compelling schedule, and providing vital packing recommendations.

Choosing the Right Time to Visit

Choosing the best time to visit Sorrento is critical because it drastically affects your overall experience. The optimal time to visit depends on your choices and interests.

1. Spring (March to May):
Spring is a fantastic time to explore Sorrento. The weather is comfortably warm, with temperatures ranging from 15°C to 20°C (59°F to 68°F). The countryside bursts with vibrant flowers, creating a colorful backdrop for your journey. It's an ideal season for outdoor activities and hiking. As a bonus, the tourist crowds are smaller, allowing for a more peaceful and authentic experience.

2. Summer (June to August):
Summer is the peak tourist season in Sorrento. The weather is hot and dry, with temperatures typically between 25°C to 30°C (77°F to 86°F). This is the perfect time for beach lovers and water enthusiasts, as the sea is warm for

swimming. However, be prepared for larger crowds and higher prices. It's advisable to book accommodations well in advance if you plan to visit during this season.

3. Autumn (September to November):
Autumn is another excellent time to visit Sorrento. The weather remains pleasant, and the summer crowds begin to dwindle. This is a perfect season for exploring historical sites, enjoying outdoor dining, and indulging in the local cuisine. With fewer tourists, you can savor a more peaceful and authentic experience.

4. Winter (December to February):
Sorrento's winter is mild but can be damp. The temperatures average between 10°C to 15°C (50°F to 59°F). While it's the off-season for tourists, it's an ideal time to enjoy a quieter, more authentic Sorrento experience. Many hotels and restaurants offer discounts during this period.

In summary, the best time to visit Sorrento depends on your interests and preferences. Each season offers unique experiences, so choose the one that aligns with what you seek from your journey.

Setting Your Budget

Before embarking on your Sorrento adventure, it's essential to establish a budget that aligns with your financial means and travel expectations. We'll provide you with estimated budgets for different traveler types, but please note that prices may vary from year to year. These budgets cover accommodation, food, transportation, activities, and souvenirs.

1. Budget Traveler:

- Accommodation: €50 - €100 per night
- Food: €20 - €40 per day (eating at local pizzerias and trattorias)

- Transportation: €20 - €40 for local transportation and day trips
- Activities: €10 - €20 per day
- Total Daily Budget: €100 - €200

2. Mid-Range Traveler:

- Accommodation: €100 - €200 per night
- Food: €40 - €80 per day (dining at a mix of restaurants)
- Transportation: €40 - €80 for local transportation and day trips
- Activities: €20 - €40 per day
- Total Daily Budget: €200 - €400

3. Luxury Traveler:

- Accommodation: €200 and above per night (luxury hotels and resorts)
- Food: €80 and above per day (fine dining)

- Transportation: €80 and above for private transportation and premium services
- Activities: €40 and above per day (exclusive experiences and guided tours)
- Total Daily Budget: €400 and above

Please keep in mind that these are approximate budget ranges, and your actual expenses may vary based on personal choices, additional activities, and the fluctuation of prices. To make the most of your budget, consider booking in advance, exploring local dining options, and prioritizing the activities and experiences that matter most to you.

Accommodation Options

Sorrento offers a wide range of accommodation options to suit various preferences and budgets. Here are some samples with updated contact information to assist you in your planning:

1. Hotel Bellevue Syrene:

- Type: Luxury 5-star hotel
- Location: Piazza della Vittoria, 5, 80067 Sorrento NA, Italy
- Contact: [Website](https://www.bellevue.it/)
- Phone: +39 081 878 1024
- Description: Hotel Bellevue Syrene offers a luxurious stay with breathtaking sea views. It features elegantly decorated rooms, a spa, and exquisite dining options.

2. Hotel Villa Fiorita:

- Type: Mid-range 3-star hotel
- Location: Via Nastro Verde, 96, 80067 Sorrento NA, Italy
- Contact: [Website](http://www.villafioritasorrento.it/)
- Phone: +39 081 878 1117
- Description: Hotel Villa Fiorita provides comfortable and affordable accommodation. It has a pool, garden, and easy access to the town center.

3. Hostel Le Sirene:

- Type: Budget hostel
- Location: Via degli Aranci, 160, 80067 Sorrento NA, Italy
- Contact: [Website](http://www.lesirenesorrento.it/)
- Phone: +39 081 878 2040
- Description: Hostel Le Sirene offers dormitory and private rooms for budget-conscious travelers. It's within walking distance of the main attractions.

4. Airbnb:

- Type: Vacation rentals
- Website: www.airbnb.com
- Description: You can find a variety of vacation rentals, apartments, and private rooms on Airbnb. It's an excellent option for those who prefer a more home-like experience.

When booking accommodation in Sorrento, consider factors such as location, amenities, and your budget. It's advisable to make reservations well in advance, especially if you plan to visit during the peak tourist season.

Creating an Itinerary

Sorrento is a treasure trove of experiences waiting to be explored. Crafting an engaging itinerary will ensure you make the most of your time in this beautiful town. Here's a sample itinerary to inspire your visit:

Day 1: Arrival in Sorrento

- Arrive in Sorrento, settle into your accommodation.
- Explore the town center, stroll along Corso Italia, and have your first taste of authentic Italian gelato.
- Dinner at a local trattoria to savor traditional Neapolitan dishes.

Day 2: Discovering Sorrento

- Morning visit to Piazza Tasso and the Chiesa di San Francesco.
- Afternoon exploration of Villa Comunale for panoramic views of the Bay of Naples.
- Evening at leisure to enjoy Sorrento's vibrant nightlife.

Day 3: Day Trip to Capri

- Take a ferry to the island of Capri.
- Explore the charming town of Capri, visit the Blue Grotto, and take a chairlift to Monte Solaro.
- Return to Sorrento in the evening.

Day 4: Exploring the Amalfi Coast

- Embark on a scenic drive or bus tour along the Amalfi Coast.

- Visit Positano, Amalfi, and Ravello to admire their stunning beauty.
- Return to Sorrento in the evening.

Day 5: Historical Sites and Culture

- Explore the archaeological site of Pompeii or Herculaneum.
- Visit the Museo Correale di Terranova to discover Sorrento's history and art.
- Evening walk along Marina Grande for a taste of local seafood cuisine.

Day 6: Leisure and Relaxation

- Spend a relaxing day at a nearby beach or the hotel's pool.
- Enjoy water activities like swimming, snorkeling, or sailing.
- Evening at leisure for shopping or additional exploration.

Day 7: Farewell Sorrento

- Take in your final moments in Sorrento with a pleasant breakfast.
- Depending on your departure time, you may have some free time to explore or purchase souvenirs.
- Depart from Sorrento with wonderful memories.

Feel free to adapt this itinerary to your interests, or mix and match activities based on your preferences. Sorrento offers a wide array of activities and attractions, ensuring there's something for every traveler.

Travel Essentials and Packing Tips

To ensure a smooth and enjoyable trip to Sorrento, here are some travel essentials and packing tips to keep in mind:

1. Passport and Travel Documents:
   - Ensure your passport is up-to-date.

- Carry a copy of your passport, travel insurance, and any necessary visas.

2. Currency:

- The official currency in Sorrento is the Euro (€). Carry some cash, but also have a credit card for convenience.

3. Electrical Adapters:

- Italy uses the Type C and F electrical plugs. Bring suitable adapters and voltage converters if needed.

4. Mobile Phone:

- Check with your mobile provider about international roaming or consider purchasing a local SIM card for data and calls.

5. Travel Insurance:

- Obtain travel insurance to cover unforeseen events like trip cancellations, medical emergencies, and lost luggage.

6. Medications:

- If you take prescription medications, ensure you have an ample supply for the trip. Carry a copy of your prescription for customs.

7. Clothing:

- Pack comfortable and breathable clothing for the Mediterranean climate. Don't forget swimwear, sunglasses, and a hat for sun protection.

8. Travel Guide and Maps:

- Bring a guidebook or use travel apps to navigate the town and its surroundings.

9. Language:

- While many in Sorrento speak English, learning a few basic Italian phrases can be helpful and respectful.

10. Personal Items:

- Remember essentials like toiletries, sunscreen, and insect repellent.

11. Adapters and Chargers:
  - Bring chargers and power banks for your devices.

12. Luggage:
  - Use lightweight and versatile luggage. A daypack for excursions is also handy.

13. Emergency Information:
  - Keep a list of important phone numbers, addresses, and local emergency contacts.

Being well-prepared and packing properly will enable you to fully enjoy your journey in Sorrento. With these essentials in tow, you can zero in on the wonders and experiences that this charming Italian town has to offer.

CHAPTER THREE:
Exploring Sorrento Neighborhoods

Marina Grande Port

Sorrento is a town with extraordinary diversity, with areas that offer a rich tapestry of history, activities, and food options. In this chapter, we'll look at four distinct areas that provide unique experiences: Sorrento's Old Town and Historic Center, Marina Grande and the Fishing Village,

Sant'Agnello and the Coastal Retreat, and Piano di Sorrento and the Lemon Groves.

Sorrento's Old Town and Historic Center

History:

Sorrento's Old Town, also known as the historic center, is the heart of the town's rich history. The area's origins can be traced back to Roman times when it was a thriving resort destination. Throughout its history, it has been shaped by various influences, including Greek, Roman, and Byzantine.

Attractions:

- Piazza Tasso: Named after the 16th-century poet Torquato Tasso, this bustling square is the center of Sorrento's social life. It's surrounded by charming cafes, restaurants, and shops.

- Corso Italia: This main street of Sorrento is known for its designer boutiques, offering an array of shopping opportunities.

- Chiesa di San Francesco: This 14th-century church is a historical gem, showcasing stunning architecture and intricate frescoes.

- Villa Comunale: This beautiful park provides panoramic views of the Bay of Naples and Mount Vesuvius.

Dining Options:

Sorrento's Old Town boasts numerous dining options. You can savor traditional Neapolitan dishes, including pizza, pasta, and seafood, at various local trattorias and restaurants. Be sure to try the local specialty, "gnocchi alla sorrentina," a delectable pasta dish with tomato sauce and melted cheese.

Marina Grande and the Fishing Village

History:

Marina Grande is Sorrento's charming fishing village, and its history is intertwined with the town's maritime heritage. It has been a hub for fishermen for centuries, known for its traditional wooden boats and colorful houses that line the shoreline.

Attractions:

- Marina Grande Beach: This is a picturesque pebble beach where you can relax, sunbathe, or take a refreshing swim in the crystal-clear waters.

- Fishing Boats: The village is still home to traditional "gozzi" fishing boats, adding to its authentic charm. You can even take a boat tour to explore the coastline.

- Waterfront Dining: Marina Grande is renowned for its seafood restaurants, offering some of the freshest catches you'll ever taste.

- Limoncello Factories: This area is famous for producing Limoncello, and you can visit one of the local factories to learn about the production process and sample this delightful lemon liqueur.

Dining Options:

Marina Grande is a seafood lover's paradise. You can indulge in a variety of fresh catches, from calamari to grilled fish, at the many waterfront restaurants. Don't forget to accompany your meal with a glass of local Limoncello.

Sant'Agnello and the Coastal Retreat

History:

Sant'Agnello, located just east of Sorrento, has its own unique history. It was a favorite resort destination in

Roman times due to its therapeutic thermal waters, and this tradition of wellness and relaxation continues today.

Attractions:

- Villa Crawford: This historic villa, built in the 1920s, is an architectural gem and offers stunning views of the Gulf of Naples.

- The Baths of Queen Joan: These thermal baths date back to Roman times and are believed to have been used by Queen Joan of Anjou. Although they are not open for bathing, they provide a fascinating glimpse into the past.

- Beaches: Sant'Agnello is known for its beautiful beaches, such as Marinella and Lido La Marinella, where you can bask in the Mediterranean sun.

Dining Options:

Sant'Agnello offers a variety of dining options, from traditional Italian restaurants to contemporary eateries. Due to its location along the coast, you can enjoy dishes featuring fresh seafood and local ingredients. Be sure to try the traditional "Scialatielli," a type of pasta native to the Campania region.

Piano di Sorrento and the Lemon Groves

History:

Piano di Sorrento, located inland from the coast, is deeply rooted in the agricultural traditions of the region. Its history is tied to the cultivation of lemons, olive groves, and vineyards.

Attractions:

- Lemon Groves: The lemon groves of Piano di Sorrento are iconic. You can visit local groves to see the lemon trees and learn about the production of Limoncello.
- Santa Maria Annunziata Church: This beautiful church, dating back to the 12th century, features stunning architecture and artwork.

- Historical Center: The town center is a delightful place to wander, with its charming streets, boutiques, and cafes.

Dining Options:

Piano di Sorrento offers a tranquil dining experience away from the bustling tourist areas. You can enjoy local dishes featuring fresh produce, including dishes with lemons, olives, and tomatoes. Don't forget to try the regional cheese, "Provolone del Monaco."

Each of Sorrento's neighborhoods provides a unique experience that reflects the town's rich history and eclectic culture. As you visit these places, you'll discover the essence of Sorrento through its historical sites, numerous attractions, and wonderful culinary options. Whether you're wandering through the Old Town, tasting seafood in Marina Grande, relaxing in Sant'Agnello, or exploring the lemon fields of Piano di Sorrento, your tour through

Sorrento's neighborhoods will be filled with fascinating encounters.

CHAPTER FOUR:
Must-See Attractions

Sorrento is a treasure mine of must-see attractions, each of which provides a unique perspective on the town's history, culture, and natural beauty. In this chapter, I'll look at some of the most famous sites and provide information about their history, location, and visiting hours.

Piazza Tasso

History:

Piazza Tasso, Sorrento's main square, is named after the town's most famous poet, Torquato Tasso. The square's vibrant atmosphere has made it the heart of social life in Sorrento for centuries.

Location:

Piazza Tasso is located at the crossroads of Sorrento's main streets, including Corso Italia and Via Fuorimura. It's easily accessible from the historic center and is a central point for exploring the town.

Visiting Hours:

- Piazza Tasso is an open public square, accessible 24/7.
- The surrounding cafes, shops, and restaurants have varying operating hours.

Amalfi Coast Road Trip

History:

The Amalfi Coast Road, or "Strada Statale 163 Amalfitana," is a historic route that dates back to the Roman era. It was originally constructed by the Romans to connect the towns of the Amalfi Coast.

Location:

The road stretches along the stunning Amalfi Coast, starting from Sorrento in the west and running all the way to Salerno in the east. It offers breathtaking views of the

Mediterranean Sea, dramatic cliffs, and picturesque coastal villages.

Visiting Hours:

- The road is accessible year-round and is best explored during daylight hours for the best views.
- Be aware that the road can be narrow and winding, so caution is essential when driving.

Sorrento Cathedral (Cattedrale dei Santi Filippo e Giacomo)

History:

The Sorrento Cathedral, dedicated to Saints Philip and James, has a rich history dating back to the 11th century. It underwent several renovations and expansions over the centuries, resulting in its stunning baroque appearance.

Location:

The cathedral is situated in the heart of Sorrento's historic center, on Corso Italia. Its prominent position makes it easily accessible and a central landmark.

Visiting Hours:

- The cathedral is open to visitors during specific hours.
- Typically, it is open from 10:00 AM to 1:00 PM and reopens from 4:00 PM to 7:00 PM, with variations on Sundays and holidays.

Museo Correale di Terranova

History:

The Museo Correale di Terranova is housed in an 18th-century villa and showcases the history and art of Sorrento. It was the former residence of the Correale family, who were prominent figures in Sorrentine society.

Location: The museum is located at Via Correale, 50, in Sorrento. It's perched on a hill overlooking the Gulf of Naples, offering stunning panoramic views.

Visiting Hours:

- The museum is open to the public with varying visiting hours. It is typically open in the mornings and afternoons but closed during lunch hours.

- Opening times can vary seasonally, so it's advisable to check in advance.

Capri Island Excursion

History:

The island of Capri has a storied history, dating back to Roman times when it was a preferred destination for the Roman elite. Its natural beauty, charming towns, and historical sites continue to attract visitors from around the world.

Location:

Capri is a short ferry ride from Sorrento, making it an accessible day trip. The island offers two main towns: Capri Town (Capri) and Anacapri.

Visiting Hours:

- Capri can be explored at your leisure. Ferries from Sorrento to Capri run regularly throughout the day.

- Be aware that some attractions on the island may have their own opening and closing hours.

Pompeii and Herculaneum

History:

Pompeii and Herculaneum are ancient Roman cities that were buried by the eruption of Mount Vesuvius in 79 AD. The well-preserved ruins offer a remarkable glimpse into daily life during the Roman Empire.

Location:

- Pompeii: Located near Naples, it is easily accessible by train or car from Sorrento.
- Herculaneum: Situated closer to Naples, it is also accessible by train or car.

Visiting Hours:
- Both Pompeii and Herculaneum have specific visiting hours and admission fees.
- Generally, they are open from morning to early evening. It's recommended to arrive early to avoid crowds.

These must-see attractions in and around Sorrento offer a rich tapestry of experiences, from historical and cultural immersion to breathtaking natural beauty. Be sure to check the specific visiting hours and any entry requirements for each attraction to make the most of your visit.

CHAPTER FIVE:
Experiencing Sorrento's Culture

Sorrento's culture is a lively one woven from centuries of history, breathtaking scenery, and the kindness of its people. This chapter will look at Sorrento's cultural components, such as the food scene, traditional cuisine, festivals and events, arts and music, and local arts and crafts.

Sorrento's Culinary Scene

Cuisine:

Sorrento's culinary scene is a testament to the rich flavors of Italian cuisine. It's renowned for its use of fresh, local ingredients, particularly lemons, tomatoes, and seafood. Dining in Sorrento is a delightful journey through the tastes of the Mediterranean.

Signature Dishes:

- Gnocchi alla Sorrentina: A mouthwatering pasta dish featuring potato gnocchi, tomato sauce, and melted cheese.

- Linguine al Limone: Linguine pasta served with a creamy lemon sauce, a nod to Sorrento's famous lemons.

- Seafood Risotto: A savory and aromatic dish showcasing the fresh catch of the day.
- Scialatielli: A type of pasta exclusive to the Campania region, typically served with a variety of sauces.

Limoncello:

Sorrento is famous for Limoncello, a lemon liqueur that embodies the essence of the town. It's made from Sorrento lemons, alcohol, sugar, and water. You can visit local Limoncello factories to witness the production process and enjoy tastings.

Dining Experience:

Sorrento offers a range of dining experiences, from casual pizzerias and trattorias to upscale restaurants. Many eateries boast breathtaking views of the sea, creating the perfect ambiance for a memorable meal.

Traditional Sorrentine Cuisine

Local Ingredients:

Sorrento's traditional cuisine is deeply rooted in the use of fresh, locally sourced ingredients. Lemons, olives, tomatoes, and herbs are staples in many dishes. Seafood, caught daily, features prominently in Sorrentine recipes.

Dishes:

- Insalata di Polipo: A refreshing octopus salad, often featuring capers, olives, and lemon dressing.

- Parmigiana di Melanzane: A classic dish made from layers of eggplant, tomato sauce, mozzarella, and Parmesan cheese.

- Pesce all'Acqua Pazza: Fish cooked "in crazy water," a flavorful broth of tomatoes, garlic, and herbs.

- Torta Caprese: A delectable chocolate and almond cake.

Wine:

Sorrento is part of the Campania region, known for its wine production. You can savor local wines like Lacryma Christi, Fiano di Avellino, and Aglianico, which pair perfectly with Sorrentine dishes.

Festivals and Events

Sorrento Film Festival:

This annual film festival celebrates cinema, featuring screenings, discussions, and cultural events.

Lemon Festival:

Sorrento's love affair with lemons culminates in the Lemon Festival, a lively event with parades, music, and lemon-themed decorations.

Settembrata Sorrentina:

A month-long celebration of Sorrentine culture and traditions, with live music, food festivals, and more.

Feast of St. Anne:
This religious festival in July features processions, fireworks, and traditional celebrations.

Sorrento Jazz Festival:
Music lovers can enjoy world-class jazz performances during this annual festival.

Arts and Music in Sorrento

Teatro Tasso:
This historic theater hosts a variety of cultural events, from classical music concerts to theatrical performances.

Local Musicians:

Sorrento has a thriving music scene, and you can often find local musicians playing traditional Neapolitan songs in the town's piazzas and restaurants.

Art Galleries:

Sorrento's art scene is thriving, with numerous galleries showcasing local and international artists.

Local Arts and Crafts

- Wood Inlay: Sorrento is renowned for its intricate wood inlay work. You can find beautifully crafted wooden boxes, furniture, and souvenirs.

- Ceramics: Hand-painted ceramics are a popular local craft. You can discover colorful plates, vases, and tiles as souvenirs.

- Lacework: The town of Sorrento is known for its lacework, including tablecloths, napkins, and clothing.

- Artisanal Perfumes: Sorrento boasts a long history of creating fragrances from local flowers and herbs, and you can find unique scents to take home.

Sorrento's culture is a delectable blend of Mediterranean delicacies, creative expression, and vibrant celebrations. You'll truly get to know this quaint Italian town by eating its traditional cuisine, experiencing its bustling cultural scene, and participating in local events. Whether you're eating Gnocchi alla Sorrentina, listening to Neapolitan music, or admiring beautiful wood inlay, Sorrento's culture will leave a lasting impression on your heart and mouth.

CHAPTER SIX:
Outdoor Adventures and Recreation

Sorrento and its surrounding area are a delight for outdoor enthusiasts. In this chapter, we'll look at the various outdoor adventures and leisure activities that await visitors to this beautiful coastal town.

Sorrento's Beaches and Water Activities

Beaches:

Sorrento offers a selection of beautiful beaches where you can bask in the Mediterranean sun and cool off in the clear waters. The most popular beaches include Marina Grande, Marina Piccola, and Meta di Sorrento.

Water Activities:

- Swimming: The warm, azure waters of the Tyrrhenian Sea are perfect for a refreshing swim.
- Snorkeling: Explore the marine life and underwater caves along the coast.

- Diving: Scuba diving enthusiasts can discover the submerged treasures of the Amalfi Coast.

- Boat Tours: Take boat tours to explore the rugged coastline, hidden coves, and the famous Blue Grotto on the island of Capri.

- Windsurfing and Kayaking: For the more adventurous, windsurfing and kayaking are popular activities along the coast.

Hiking in the Sorrento Peninsula

The Sorrento Peninsula:

This area is a hiker's paradise, offering a network of picturesque trails with panoramic views of the sea and cliffs. Popular hiking routes include:

- Path of the Gods (Sentiero degli Dei): This trail offers breathtaking views of the Amalfi Coast.

- Valle delle Ferriere: Explore the natural beauty of this lush valley.

- Punta Campanella: Hike to the tip of the Sorrento Peninsula for stunning vistas.

Exploring Mount Vesuvius

Mount Vesuvius:

A visit to Sorrento provides a unique opportunity to explore one of the most famous volcanoes in the world. You can hike to the summit of Mount Vesuvius, where you'll witness panoramic views of the Bay of Naples and gain insight into the volcanic forces that shaped this region.

Hiking to the Crater:

The hike to the crater is a moderate but rewarding experience. Local guides offer insights into the volcano's history and geology.

Visiting Hours:

Mount Vesuvius is typically open to visitors year-round, although weather conditions can affect accessibility. It's advisable to check in advance.

Golfing near Sorrento

Golf Clubs:

The region around Sorrento is home to several golf courses. One of the most notable is the Sorrento Golf Club. Nestled between the sea and the hills, this golf course offers a challenging and picturesque round of golf.

Scenic Fairways:

Golfers can enjoy stunning views of the Gulf of Naples while teeing off on this 18-hole course.

Island Hopping in the Gulf of Naples

Capri:

A short ferry ride from Sorrento takes you to the enchanting island of Capri. Explore the island's charming towns, visit the Blue Grotto, and take in stunning sea views from the Gardens of Augustus.

Ischia:

Known for its thermal springs and beautiful beaches, Ischia is another island worth exploring. You can soak in natural thermal pools or explore the Aragonese Castle.

Procida:
This quaint island offers colorful houses, vibrant fishing harbors, and a serene atmosphere, making it a perfect day trip destination.

Day Trips to Positano and Ravello

Positano:
Known for its dramatic cliffside houses and winding streets, Positano is a picturesque town along the Amalfi Coast. Stroll along its beaches, shop for local crafts, and dine in charming restaurants.

Ravello:

Perched high in the hills, Ravello offers stunning gardens, historic villas, and classical music festivals. Visit the Villa Rufolo and Villa Cimbrone for breathtaking views.

Sorrento's natural beauty, from its stunning beaches to its hiking trails, offers endless possibilities for outdoor adventures. Whether you're exploring the ancient ruins of Mount Vesuvius, enjoying a round of golf, or embarking on island-hopping excursions, the town and its surroundings provide a wealth of recreational activities for visitors to experience and savor.

CHAPTER SEVEN:
Sorrento for Every Traveler

Sorrento welcomes tourists of all ages and interests. In this chapter, we will look at what Sorrento has to offer different types of travelers, including families, lovers, retirees, tourists, students, and solo explorers.

Family-Friendly Activities

Sorrento is an ideal destination for family vacations, offering a wide range of activities suitable for all ages:

- Beach Days: Spend quality time on Sorrento's family-friendly beaches, such as Marina Grande, where the calm waters are perfect for children to swim and play.

- Lemon Tours: Kids will be fascinated by tours of lemon groves, where they can learn about Sorrento's famous lemons and even try their hand at making lemon-based treats.

- Boat Tours: Family-friendly boat tours are a great way to explore the coastline and enjoy swimming and snorkeling in the crystal-clear waters.

- Pompeii and Herculaneum: Introduce your children to history by taking them to the nearby archaeological sites of Pompeii and Herculaneum, where they can walk in the footsteps of ancient Romans.

Sorrento for Romance

Sorrento's natural beauty and intimate atmosphere make it a perfect destination for couples in search of romance:

- Sunset Views: Savor stunning sunsets over the Bay of Naples while strolling along the clifftop promenades or dining at a sea-view restaurant.

- Private Boat Trips: Enjoy a private boat tour to explore secluded coves and the romantic island of Capri.

- Wine Tasting: Share a romantic evening sampling local wines at a vineyard overlooking the sea.

- Candlelit Dinners: Sorrento offers a multitude of restaurants with intimate settings where you can enjoy exquisite Italian cuisine together.

Sorrento for Seniors

Sorrento's gentle pace, mild climate, and cultural richness make it a wonderful destination for seniors:

- Historical Sites: Explore the town's historical sites, including the Cathedral, the Museum of Correale, and the ancient walls, all accessible on leisurely walks.

- Thermal Baths: Relax in the soothing thermal baths of Sant'Agnello and enjoy the rejuvenating effects of the natural waters.

- Local Crafts: Seniors can appreciate the town's artisanal traditions, such as lacework and wood inlay, which make for unique souvenirs.

- Easy Day Trips: Take short, comfortable day trips to nearby destinations like Capri, Pompeii, or the Amalfi Coast.

Sorrento for Tourists

Sorrento caters to tourists with its well-established infrastructure and an array of attractions:

- Shopping: Tourists can indulge in retail therapy along Corso Italia, where designer boutiques and local shops abound.

- Museums and Galleries: Visit the Museo Correale di Terranova, art galleries, and the town's historic buildings to immerse yourself in Sorrento's cultural heritage.

- Day Tours: Join guided day tours to Pompeii, Herculaneum, Capri, and the Amalfi Coast, ensuring a hassle-free exploration of the region.

- Culinary Delights: Savor authentic Italian cuisine in local trattorias, pizzerias, and seafood restaurants.

Sorrento for Students

Sorrento offers an enriching experience for students, with opportunities to learn about history, culture, and local traditions:

- Archaeological Excursions: Study ancient history by exploring the ruins of Pompeii and Herculaneum, where you can witness the daily life of ancient Romans.

- Language Courses: Enroll in Italian language courses to immerse yourself in the local culture and communicate with residents.

- Local Cuisine: Participate in cooking classes to learn how to prepare traditional dishes like gnocchi alla Sorrentina or Limoncello.

- Outdoor Adventures: Engage in outdoor activities such as hiking, water sports, and boat tours to experience the region's natural beauty.

Solo Travel Tips and Safety

Solo travelers can enjoy Sorrento's beauty while staying safe and making the most of their journey:

- Safety: Sorrento is generally considered a safe destination, but it's advisable to take standard precautions like securing your belongings and being aware of your surroundings.

- Meet Locals: Embrace the opportunity to meet locals and fellow travelers. Engage in conversations at cafes, join group tours, or attend local events.

- Learn Some Italian: While many in Sorrento speak English, learning a few basic Italian phrases can enhance your experience and help you communicate more effectively.

- Day Trips: Join group day trips to nearby attractions. It's a great way to explore the region while having company during your travels.

Sorrento's diversity makes it an appealing destination for people of different origins and interests. Whether you're on a family holiday, a romantic getaway, a senior retreat, a tourist adventure, a student excursion, or a solo journey, Sorrento has something unique to offer that will make your visit memorable and rewarding.

CHAPTER EIGHT: Practical Information and Resources

A successful journey to Sorrento, Italy, requires practical knowledge and useful resources. This chapter contains information about money and currencies, language and communication, safety and health precautions, sustainable travel in Sorrento, and important contacts and emergency numbers.

Money and Currency

- Currency: The official currency in Sorrento is the Euro (€).

- Banking: ATMs are widely available, and you can find banks and exchange offices in the town center. Major credit cards, such as Visa and Mastercard, are generally accepted in hotels, restaurants, and shops. However, it's a good idea to carry some cash for smaller establishments.

Language and Communication

- Italian: The official language of Sorrento is Italian. While most locals working in the tourism industry speak some English, it's helpful to learn a few basic Italian phrases to enhance your experience and show respect for the local culture.

- Translation Apps: Consider using translation apps like Google Translate to assist with communication.

Safety and Health Tips

- Safety: Sorrento is generally a safe destination for travelers. However, exercise standard precautions like safeguarding your belongings and being aware of your surroundings. Avoid leaving valuables unattended on beaches or in rental cars.

- Healthcare: Medical services in Sorrento are of high quality. Ensure you have comprehensive travel insurance with coverage for medical emergencies. Note that it's essential to have travel insurance that covers any outdoor activities you plan to undertake.

- Sun Protection: The Mediterranean sun can be intense. Protect yourself from sunburn by wearing sunscreen, sunglasses, and a hat.

- Water: The tap water in Sorrento is generally safe to drink, but some travelers prefer bottled water.

- Emergency Numbers: In case of emergencies, the following numbers may be helpful:
  - Police: 113
  - Medical Emergency: 118
  - Fire Department: 115

Sustainable Travel in Sorrento

Sustainable travel practices not only benefit the environment but also enhance your experience in Sorrento. Consider these tips:

- Public Transportation: Use local buses, trams, or trains to reduce your carbon footprint when exploring the area.

- Walking and Cycling: Sorrento and its surroundings are ideal for walking and cycling. Opt for eco-friendly modes of transportation to explore the town and its beautiful coast.

- Recycle and Conserve: Dispose of waste responsibly by using recycling bins and conserving water and energy in accommodations.

- Support Local: Purchase locally made products and support businesses that focus on sustainability and responsible tourism.

Useful Contacts and Emergency Numbers

- Tourist Information:

  - Sorrento Tourist Office:

    - Address: Via Luigi de Maio, 35, 80067 Sorrento NA, Italy

    - Phone: +39 081 8074033

    - Email: info@sorrentotourism.com

- Embassies and Consulates:

  - If you need to contact your country's embassy or consulate while in Sorrento, inquire at the nearest embassy office in Naples.

- Emergency Numbers:

  - For emergencies in Sorrento, dial 112 for police, medical assistance, or the fire department.

Having this practical information at your fingertips will help you have a safe and enjoyable visit to Sorrento, enabling you to focus on exploring the stunning Amalfi Coast, savoring Italian cuisine, and immersing yourself in the local culture.

APPENDIX

Useful Travel Resources

To make your trip to Sorrento, Italy, as seamless and pleasurable as possible, you must have access to useful travel tools. This appendix has a variety of useful tools, including travel apps, a Sorrento trip checklist, currency and banking information, and Italian phrases and so on.

Helpful Travel Apps

1. Google Maps: This versatile app can assist you in navigating Sorrento and its surroundings. You can download offline maps, which come in handy when you're in areas with limited internet connectivity.

2. XE Currency Converter: Stay updated on currency exchange rates with this handy app, ensuring you always know the value of the Euro.

3. TripAdvisor: Use this app to find recommendations for restaurants, accommodations, and attractions in Sorrento based on traveler reviews.

4. Rome2rio: Plan your transportation within Sorrento and nearby cities with this app. It provides information on buses, trains, and other transportation options.

5. Duolingo: If you'd like to brush up on your Italian language skills, this app offers free lessons in a fun and interactive format.

Sorrento Travel Checklist

- Passport and visa (if required).
- Travel insurance with medical coverage.
- Euros (€) for small expenses, such as transportation and snacks.
- Credit/debit cards for larger purchases.
- Printed copies of accommodation reservations.

- Weather-appropriate clothing and comfortable walking shoes.
- Power adapter for Type C and Type F electrical outlets.
- Mobile phone with international roaming or local SIM card.
- Personal toiletries and medications.
- Necessary travel documents and photocopies.
- Reusable water bottle and sun protection (hat, sunscreen, sunglasses).
- Camera and accessories.
- Public transportation schedules and maps.

Currency and Banking Information

- Currency: The official currency in Sorrento is the Euro (€).

- Banking: ATMs are readily available throughout Sorrento, especially in the town center. Most major credit and debit cards, such as Visa and Mastercard, are widely accepted in hotels, restaurants, and shops. However, it's wise to have some cash on hand for smaller establishments and for places with limited card acceptance.

Having these resources on hand will help you navigate Sorrento with ease, access valuable information, and make the most of your Italian coastal adventure. Whether you're exploring the charming town, enjoying local cuisine, or taking in the stunning views along the Amalfi Coast, these tools will enhance your travel experience.

Italian Phrases and Pronunciation Guide

Mastering a few basic Italian phrases can greatly enrich your experience while traveling in Sorrento, Italy. In this language guide, you'll find essential phrases for travelers, ordering food and drinks, and navigating public transportation. We've included pronunciation tips to help you communicate effectively.

Basic Phrases for Travelers

1. Hello: Ciao (CHOW)

2. Good morning: Buongiorno (BWOHN-JOHR-noh)

3. Good afternoon: Buon pomeriggio (BWOHN poh-meh-REE-djoh)

4. Good evening: Buona sera (BWOH-nah SEH-rah)

5. Goodbye: Arrivederci (ah-ree-veh-DEHR-chee)

6. Please: Per favore (PEHR FAH-voh-reh)

7. Thank you: Grazie (GRAH-tsye)

8. Yes: Sì (SEE)

9. No: No (NOH)

10. Excuse me: Scusi (SKOO-zee)

11. I'm sorry: Mi dispiace (MEE dees-pee-AH-che)

12. Do you speak English?: Parla inglese? (PAHR-lah een-GLEH-zeh?)

13. I don't understand: Non capisco (NOHN kah-PEES-koh)

14. Help: Aiuto (ah-YOO-toh)

15. Where is...?: Dov'è...? (doh-VEH...?)

16. How much does this cost?: Quanto costa questo? (KWAHN-toh KOHS-tah KWEH-stoh?)

17. I need a doctor: Ho bisogno di un dottore (oh bee-SOH-nyoh dee oon doht-TOH-reh)

18. I'm lost: Sono perso/a (SOH-noh PEHR-soh/ah)

Ordering Food and Drinks

19. Menu, please: Il menu, per favore (eel MEH-noo, pehr fah-VOH-reh)

20. I would like...: Vorrei... (VOHR-rey...)

21. Water: Acqua (AH-kwah)

22. Coffee: Caffè (KAH-feh)

23. Tea: Tè (TEH)

24. Beer: Birra (BEER-rah)

25. Wine: Vino (VEE-noh)

26. Bread: Pane (PAH-neh)

27. Meat: Carne (KAHR-neh)

28. Fish: Pesce (PEH-sheh)

29. Vegetarian: Vegetariano/a (veh-jeh-TAH-ryah-noh/ah)

30. Check, please: Il conto, per favore (eel KOHN-toh, pehr fah-VOH-reh)

31. Delicious: Delizioso/a (deh-lee-TSYOH-soh/ah)

Navigating Public Transportation

32. Bus stop: Fermata dell'autobus (fehr-MAH-tah dehl AOO-toh-boos)

33. Bus station: Stazione dell'autobus (stah-TSYOH-neh dehl AOO-toh-boos)

34. Train station: Stazione ferroviaria (stah-TSYOH-neh fehr-roh-vee-AH-ryah)

35. Ticket: Biglietto (bee-LYEHT-toh)

36. One ticket to...: Un biglietto per... (oon bee-LYEHT-toh pehr...)

37. Is this the right bus/train?: È questo il bus/treno giusto? (eh KWEHS-toh eel boos/TREH-noh JYOO-stoh?)

38. How much is a ticket to...?: Quanto costa un biglietto per...? (KWAHN-toh KOHS-tah oon bee-LYEHT-toh pehr...?)

39. When does the bus/train to... leave?: A che ora parte il bus/treno per...? (ah keh OH-rah PAR-teh eel boos/TREH-noh pehr...?)

40. Where is the bus/train station?: Dov'è la stazione dell'autobus/treno? (doh-VEH lah stah-TSYOH-neh dehl AOO-toh-boos/TREH-noh?)

Learning these Italian words will not only enhance your visit to Sorrento, but also show your appreciation for the local culture. The people of Sorrento will appreciate your efforts to engage with their language, even if you primarily communicate in English throughout your visit.

Map to Sorrento

Made in the USA
Monee, IL
22 October 2024